Exploring the Old Dominion, A Journey Through Historic Virginia From the Coast to the Mountains

Table of Contents

INTRODUCTION

Welcome to the Old Dominion: Exploring Virginia's Rich Heritage and Natural Beauty

The "Old Dominion," sometimes referred to as Virginia, is a mesmerizing location that entices visitors with its extensive history, dynamic culture, and spectacular natural beauty. This ancient state, which is located along the eastern coast of the United States, provides a wide variety of experiences, from its picturesque coastal vistas to its spectacular mountain ranges.

You are welcome to tour around Virginia through this thorough travel guide, exploring the undiscovered gems and savoring its enduring appeal.

The Historical Legacy of Virginia

Explore Virginia's historical sights and landmarks as you delve into the origins of the United States. From the splendor of Monticello, Thomas Jefferson's famous mansion, to the historic triangle of Jamestown, Williamsburg, and Yorktown, where the cornerstones of American democracy were placed, Virginia is a live reminder of the history of the country.

Outdoor Splendors and Natural Wonders

Discover the breathtaking splendor of Virginia's unspoiled countryside. Enter Shenandoah National Park to find lush woods, gushing waterfalls, and expansive views. Find out more about the captivating Blue Ridge Mountains and the Appalachian Trail, which provide many chances for hiking, camping, and animal encounters.

Virginia's natural treasures will wow you whether you're visiting coastal reserves, wandering through quaint tiny towns, or taking in the state's unique flora and animals.

Dynamic Cities and Cultural Gems

Cities and cultural centers of Virginia are thriving and diversified, providing a unique blend of history, art, music, and gastronomic pleasures. Explore the state's capital's attractive streets to discover a mix of stunning architecture, hip districts, and a bustling cultural scene.

Discover Norfolk's creative flair, a coastal city renowned for its top-notch museums and exciting events. Discover Charlottesville's diverse cultural heritage, which includes major educational institutions, historical landmarks, and a developing wine area.

Seaside Escapes and Coastal Charms

Miles of immaculate beaches, quaint coastal communities, and an abundance of leisure opportunities surround Virginia's coastline. Discover Virginia Beach's busy beachfront, where the sand, surf, and vibrant boardwalk provide limitless amusement. Learn about Chincoteague Island's peace, which is known for its wild ponies and untouched natural beauty. Explore Norfolk's rich maritime history, which includes the presence of the magnificent Battleship Wisconsin.

Gastronomic Delights and Regional flavors

The culinary scene of Virginia is a mouthwatering blend of coastal seafood, Southern cuisine, and farm-to-table dining. Enjoy delectable meals including Virginia ham, crab cakes from the Chesapeake Bay, and traditional Southern comfort cuisine.

Explore Virginia's developing wine districts, which are renowned for producing wines that have won awards, and enjoy the fruits of the state's vineyards. Virginia gives food lovers a delicious voyage with culinary festivals, craft brewers, and artisanal food markets.

This trip manual will be your dependable travel companion as you set out to explore Virginia. It offers priceless insights, useful advice, and thorough details on the state's attractions, lodgings, transportation, and safety.

Prepare to learn about the fascinating tales, stunning scenery, and undiscovered wonders that make Virginia such a memorable travel destination. Let the Old Dominion capture your heart as you make priceless memories exploring Virginia's rich history and stunning scenery.

II. GETTING READY FOR YOUR TRIP

Weather and Best Times to Visit Guide

Virginia has a variety of climates throughout the year, and each season has its attractions and activities. Here is a list of the seasons, along with information on what to anticipate in terms of weather and when to go:

April to June:

Virginia blooms with vivid flowers and lush vegetation in the spring, making it a lovely time to go there.

- With typical highs ranging from the 60s°F (15-20°C) in April to the 80s°F (25-30°C) in June, temperatures throughout this season are pleasant to warm.

- Outdoor pursuits like hiking, seeing gardens, and taking leisurely drives around the countryside are quite popular in the spring.

- In the spring, it's a good idea to bring layers since the temperature might change during the day.

Summertime (June through August)

In Virginia, summer means warm to scorching temperatures and increased humidity, especially near the shore.
- With occasional heat waves exceeding 100s°F (38°C), average high temperatures vary from the 80s°F (25–30°C) to the 90s°F (30–35°C).

- Water sports on rivers and lakes as well as beach activities along the shore are best enjoyed in the summer.
- To shield yourself from the sun's rays, it is a good idea to bring lightweight,

breathable clothes, sunscreen, and a hat.

September to November:

Virginia's stunning autumn foliage makes it one of the top places to go throughout the fall.

- In September, the typical high temperature is in the 70s°F (20–25°C), and by November, it has dropped to the 50s°F (10–15°C).

- Hiking, collecting apples, and picturesque drives along the Blue Ridge Parkway are just a few of the outdoor pursuits that may be enjoyed in the great outdoors as a result of the changing hues of the leaves.

- In the autumn, it is advised to bring layers since temperatures might change, particularly in hilly places.

December through February is winter.

Virginia has colder winters, especially in the state's hilly areas.

- From the 40s°F (5-10°C) in December to the 50s°F (10-15°C) in February, the average high-temperature ranges.

- Winters are warmer at the coast than they are in the mountains, where snowfall is more frequent.

- In the Appalachian Mountains, wintertime provides chances for skiing, snowboarding, and other winter sports.

- Packing warm clothes is crucial, so make sure you have a coat, hat, gloves, and the right shoes for any potential snowfall.

Overall, your interests and the activities you want to do will determine when is the ideal time to visit Virginia. Generally speaking, spring and autumn are preferred because of the nice weather, in bloom flowers, and bright foliage. While winter draws those looking for winter experiences and snowy vistas, summer is the best season for beachgoers and water sports aficionados.

To make sure you're ready for the circumstances during your stay, don't forget to check the precise weather forecast for your desired trip dates and Virginian locations.

Packing Tips for Your Adventure

It's crucial to pack thoughtfully while getting ready for your Virginia excursion to make sure you have everything you need for a relaxing and pleasurable trip. To help you make the most of your trip, consider the following packing advice:

- **Check the Weather:** Before you pack, look up the weather predictions for the whole period of your vacation as well as the particular Virginia places you'll be visiting. This will enable you to pack the proper apparel and equipment.

- **Layering Clothes:** Because Virginia weather may be unpredictable, it's advisable to carry layers of clothing. This enables you to adapt to the day's shifting temperatures. Bring breathable, light clothes for warm days, and add layers of waterproof clothing, jackets, or sweaters for chilly or rainy weather.

- Pack comfortable walking shoes or hiking boots, particularly if you want to explore Virginia's picturesque trails or metropolitan neighborhoods. Bring sandals or flip-flops if you want to visit the beach or take a leisurely walk.

- **Outdoor Gear:** Bring the necessary equipment, such as a daypack, water bottles, sunscreen, insect repellant, and a hat for sun protection, if you want to engage in outdoor activities like hiking or camping. Keep a durable pair of sunglasses in your bag to protect your eyes from the sun.

- **Rain Gear:** Because Virginia sometimes experiences rain, it's a good idea to take a lightweight rain jacket or a waterproof shell to keep you dry. It might also be helpful to have an umbrella or a portable rain poncho.

- Carry your necessary equipment, like a smartphone, camera, or tablet, as well as the corresponding chargers. To guarantee you have backup power for your gadgets when traveling, think about bringing a power bank.

- **Travel adapter:** If you're coming from another country, don't forget to bring one with you so you can charge your electronics and make sure they work with U.S. electrical outlets.

- **Medication and First Aid Kit:** Pack enough prescription medication to last the length of your vacation if you take any. A basic first aid package that includes materials like bandages, painkillers, and any personal prescriptions or treatments you may need is another thing you might want to carry.

- Bring your trip essentials, such as your passport, ID, and any required visas or information on travel insurance, along with your travel documentation, which should include these items. Keep them in a location that is both safe and convenient.

- Pack toiletries, shampoo, conditioner, soap, and toothpaste in travel sizes together with other personal things. Bring a small towel, a reusable water bottle, and any other personal things you think you'll need for a pleasant trip.

- **Snacks and Water:** Having snacks and a water bottle on hand may be useful when touring Virginia, particularly during outdoor activities or lengthy rides. To stay energized during the day, bring along some non-perishable foods like energy bars, almonds, or dried fruit.

Keep in mind to travel light and just carry what is necessary. whether you want to lighten your baggage, ask your lodging whether it offers extras like towels, hairdryers, or toiletries.

III. DISCOVERING VIRGINIA'S COASTAL GEMS

Virginia Beach: Sun, Sand, and Oceanic Delights.

Virginia Beach, which is a top beach resort with a great balance of sun, sand, and water pleasures, is situated on Virginia's southeast coast. This dynamic city welcomes guests to participate in a variety of outdoor activities, gastronomic pleasures, and a thriving beach culture thanks to its immaculate beachfront that stretches for kilometers along the Atlantic Ocean. The experiences Virginia Beach has to offer are described in detail below:

Gorgeous Beaches:

- Beach lovers and sunbathers are drawn to Virginia Beach by its beautiful coastline and soft, sand beaches.

- Visitors may enjoy the sun, cool off in the surf, play beach games, and participate in watersports on the main beach, often known as the Virginia Beach Oceanfront.

- A three-mile boardwalk that is well-kept and offers beautiful vistas, exciting entertainment, and a variety of stores, restaurants, and activities complements the beach.

Outdoor Activities:

Beyond its beautiful beaches, Virginia Beach has a wide range of outdoor activities for nature enthusiasts and thrill seekers.

- Discover the different ecosystems of the Back Bay National Wildlife Refuge, a beautiful coastal refuge that includes marshes, dunes, and forests. Explore the refuge's pathways on foot or by bicycle to see a variety of animals and migrating birds.

- Virginia Beach offers great conditions for kayaking, fishing, paddle boarding, and surfing for fans of water activities. The city is a well-liked location for boat cruises and dolphin-watching excursions.

Gastronomic Delights

With a concentration on seafood and beach fare, Virginia Beach has a thriving food scene.
- At beachfront eateries and seafood shacks, savor delicious crabs, oysters, and regional fish that have just been caught.

- Discover the ambiance of Creative District to sample a variety of cuisines, farm-to-table treats, and craft brews from nearby breweries. The area is recognized for its artistic ambiance and unusual eating choices.

Aquarium and Marine Science Center of Virginia:

- Explore the Virginia Aquarium and Marine Science Center in Virginia Beach to learn more about the marvels of the ocean.

- Through interactive displays, including a walk-through tunnel where you can see sharks, stingrays, and other aquatic animals up close, learn about the wonderful world of marine life.

- The aquarium also provides stimulating experiences for guests of all ages with educational programs, live animal displays, and outdoor nature walks.

Entertainment and Festivals:

- The year-round program of events and festivals in Virginia Beach provides excitement and a touch of culture to your stay.

- Attend the Neptune Festival, a well-liked yearly occasion honoring the city's maritime history, which will include live music, art exhibits, sand sculpture contests, and a spectacular procession.

- The Veterans United Home Loans Amphitheater is an outdoor facility where you can see live performances and concerts by well-known performers.

Military Background

Due to its proximity to military bases and long military-related history, Virginia Beach has significant links to the armed services.

- Visit the Military Aviation Museum to get insight into the region's aviation history while seeing a unique collection of antique aircraft from World Wars I and II.

- Investigate the Naval Aviation Monument Park, which celebrates American achievements. pilots in the Navy and Marine Corps.

Everyone can enjoy the lively beachfront experience that Virginia Beach has to offer. This seaside location will wow you with its natural beauty, vibrant atmosphere, and kind hospitality whether you're looking for beach relaxation, exhilarating outdoor activities, mouthwatering seafood, or cultural entertainment. Create enduring memories of your seaside trip by immersing yourself in the sun, sand, and marine pleasures that Virginia Beach has to offer.

Chincoteague Island: Discovering Wildlife and Seaside Charm

Chincoteague Island, located off the eastern coast of Virginia, is a charming vacation spot renowned for its beautiful beaches, variety of species, and laid-back coastal appeal. This barrier island draws tourists from near and far with its special combination of natural beauty, outdoor experiences, and a close-knit community. It is located just off the coast of the Delmarva Peninsula. Here is a thorough examination of Chincoteague Island and the adventures you might expect:

<u>National Wildlife Refuge at Chincoteague:</u>

- The Chincoteague National Wildlife Refuge, a protected area with approximately 14,000 acres of dunes, marshes, and maritime woods, is the gem of Chincoteague Island.

- In addition to providing a haven for migrating birds including the famous Chincoteague ponies, herons, eagles, and more than 300 kinds of birds, the refuge is noted for its unique environment.

- Discover the beautiful routes of the refuge, such as the Animal Loop and Swan Cove Trail, which provide chances for animal and bird viewing as well as breath-taking vistas of the surroundings.

Assateague Island:

Assateague Island, a barrier island famous for its natural beauty, is joined to Chincoteague Island by a brief causeway.

- Admire the renowned Chincoteague ponies, a group of wild horses who wander without restriction around the island. It is an incredible pleasure to see these magnificent animals grazing in their natural environment.

- Enjoy Assateague Island's gorgeous beaches, which are great for surfing, swimming, tanning, beachcombing, and more. To save the delicate coastal ecology, follow the norms and regulations.

Pony Penning and Pony Swim:

The annual Pony Swim and Pony Penning competition on Chincoteague Island, which takes place in July, is well-known.
- Observe the sight as local wranglers help the famed Chincoteague horses swim across the Assateague Channel. This occasion draws tourists from all over the globe and provides a special

look into the island's extensive equestrian past.

- Following the swim, the ponies are collected and sold at auction to raise money for the Chincoteague Volunteer Fire Company, enhancing the feeling of camaraderie and celebration on the island.

Beaches and Outside Activities:

Chincoteague Island has immaculate, empty beaches that provide a peaceful coastal vacation. Enjoy the sun and the soothing seaside breezes while unwinding on the sandy coastlines.

- Try your hand at several outdoor activities, including kayaking, canoeing, paddleboarding, and fishing in the nearby seas. Discover the tranquil estuaries and streams that are rich with wildlife and other natural beauties.

- Explore the island at your leisure by renting a bicycle or going on a picturesque boat excursion. Enjoy Chincoteague Island's gorgeous scenery, quaint seaside homes, and breathtaking views that make it a haven for wildlife enthusiasts.

History and Culture of the sea:

Visit the Museum of Chincoteague Island to fully appreciate the rich maritime heritage and culture of the island. Learn about the island's maritime history with displays on the fishing industry, boatbuilding, and oyster and clam industries.

- Explore the picturesque downtown area, which is dotted with tiny boutiques, art galleries, and restaurants dishing up local delicacies and fresh seafood. Try delicious seafood specialties including oysters, clams, and other seafood dishes that are characteristic of the island's culinary scene.

Annual Celebrations and Events

Annual festivals and activities on Chincoteague Island highlight the island's distinctive personality and sense of community.

- Don't miss the Chincoteague Seafood Festival, where you can enjoy a delectable selection of regional seafood delicacies, live music, and fun activities for the whole family.

- Learn more about the island's oyster tradition at the Chincoteague Oyster Festival, which features oyster shucking competitions, tastings, and displays.

- Indulge in the natural beauties and quaint island lifestyle of Chincoteague

Island, which provides the ideal fusion of animal encounters, coastline scenery, and a laid-back environment. Chincoteague Island guarantees a wonderful and alluring coastal retreat, whether you want to explore the animal preserve, take in the famed Pony Swim, or just unwind on the beaches.

Historic Jamestown: Discovering America's Colonial Roots

Historic Jamestown is a fascinating location that transports you back in time to the very beginnings of America's colonial history. It is located along the banks of the James River in Virginia. Jamestown boasts enormous historical importance as the first permanent English colony in the New World and provides a multitude of sights and educational opportunities. The colonial origins you may follow via Historic Jamestown are explored in depth here:

<u>Jamestown Colony</u>:

- Start your trip with Jamestown Settlement, a living history museum that offers an in-depth look at early colonial life in America.

- Step into a Powhatan Indian village that has been faithfully rebuilt so that you may discover more about the local native population and speak with costumed interpreters who will help you understand their culture and customs.

- Discover reproductions of the Susan Constant, Godspeed, and Discovery, the three ships that carried the English settlers to Jamestown. Learn about the challenging circumstances the colonists experienced while traveling across the Atlantic.

Historic Jamestowne

- Visit Historic Jamestowne, a National Historic Site administered by the Association for the Preservation of Virginia Antiquities and the National Park Service.

- Learn about the original location of the Jamestown colony, where archaeologists are still discovering amazing relics and piecing together historical accounts.

- Visit the archaeological museum and the Archaearium to see important objects found at the location, such as the ruins of the old fort, tools, ceramics, and early settlers' items.

Jamestown Island:

- Discover Jamestown Island's natural splendor, which includes the historic district and provides beautiful trails and panoramas.

- Take a leisurely walk through the pathways on the island to take in the peace and beautiful surroundings that previously saw the hardships and successes of the early colonists.

- The island is home to a wide variety of animals and migrating bird species, so keep a watch out for them.

Project for the Rediscovery of Jamestown's Archaeology:

- Learn more about the Jamestown Rediscovery Archaeological Project Is ongoing archaeological investigations and findings.

- Attend enlightening talks and tours offered by historians and archaeologists who discuss their research and discoveries about the early colony and its residents.

- Learn about new findings, such as the identification of notable people and the tales they tell about life in the settlement's early years.

Programs for Historical Interpretation

- Participate in the numerous historical interpretation events available at Jamestown, including agricultural demonstrations from the 17th century, musket shooting exhibitions, and hands-on exhibits that let visitors experience colonial life.

- Attend costumed living history events when reenactors take on the roles of historical individuals and converse with guests about the struggles and accomplishments of the early settlers.

Efforts made in preservation and conservation

- Beyond its historical importance, Jamestown is significant because it is the focus of current restoration and conservation efforts.

- Discover the steps taken to save the archaeological relics, historic buildings, and surrounding ecosystems so that future generations may continue to study and benefit from this significant aspect of American history.

A fascinating look into the origins of America's colonial legacy may be found in Historic Jamestown. Visitors may fully immerse themselves in the successes and difficulties experienced by the early settlers via the model ships and live history exhibitions at Jamestown Settlement and the archaeological discoveries at Historic

Jamestowne. You'll get a greater knowledge of the people and occasions that molded the country we know today as you explore America's colonial past.

Norfolk: A Vibrant City with Maritime Heritage

Norfolk, a thriving city in southeast Virginia, is a perfect example of how to combine a historic maritime tradition with a contemporary urban appeal. Norfolk has long been a center of maritime activity and cultural variety since it is situated along the scenic Chesapeake Bay and boasts one of the greatest natural harbors in the world. Here is a comprehensive analysis of Norfolk and the activities it provides, highlighting its marine history and energetic city life:

Norfolk Harbor:

- Explore Norfolk Harbor first as it serves as the city's entry point to its maritime history. Observe the humming bustle of ships, barges, and sailboats making their way across the harbor's deep waters.

- Walk along the waterfront promenade, which is surrounded by parks, marinas, and picturesque vistas. Take in the expansive views of the harbor and the stunning skyline, which features both old-world and contemporary architectural wonders.

The Nauticus and Wisconsin Battleship

- Visit Nauticus, a thrilling maritime-themed museum situated on the downtown waterfront, to get fully immersed in Norfolk's nautical heritage.

- Learn about naval science, maritime trade, and the significance of the Chesapeake Bay environment via interactive displays. Don't miss the magnificent display of the Battleship Wisconsin, one of the biggest and last battleships constructed by the United States. Navy.

- Discover the Battleship Wisconsin's decks, discover its fascinating history, and get insight into what it was like to serve as a sailor on board this magnificent ship.

The Chrysler Art Museum:

- The Chrysler Museum of Art, known for its extensive collection of more than 30,000 pieces spanning 5,000 years of history, enhances Norfolk's cultural landscape.

- Enjoy the museum's wide collection of paintings, sculptures, decorative arts, and glasswork that includes both European and American art. A notable feature is the glass collection, which includes works by famous glass artists like Dale Chihuly.

- To contribute to Norfolk's thriving arts and cultural scene, the museum regularly sponsors transient exhibits, educational programs, and community activities.

Waterside District:

- Discover the vibrant atmosphere of the Waterside District, a cluster of restaurants, shops, and entertainment venues located on the riverfront.

- Enjoy a variety of cuisines, from foreign fare to regional seafood delicacies, while eating on the riverside and taking in the beautiful Elizabeth River scenery.

- Live music performances, festivals, and other seasonal events are also held in the Waterside District, making it a lively and interesting gathering place for both residents and tourists.

Neon District:

- Discover the Neon District in Norfolk, a flourishing arts neighborhood where the streets are alive with vivid art installations, colorful murals, and modern galleries.

- Marvel at the outdoor art scene, where murals grace the walls of buildings and show off the city's dedication to fostering cultural expression and creativity.

- Engage with local artists, and visit regional galleries, and studios to fully experience the vibrant arts scene that is defining the character of the city.

Events and Festivals:

- Throughout the year, Norfolk presents a program of exciting festivals and events to honor its maritime history, diversity of cultures, and thriving community.

- Don't miss the Harborfest, an event that honors Norfolk's maritime history every year and includes fireworks, live music, parades of tall ships, and other family-friendly activities.

- Other noteworthy occasions include the Virginia Arts Festival, which showcases top-notch performances in music, theater, and dance, and the Norfolk NATO Festival, which promotes international relations by exhibiting other cultures.

The ethos of a thriving coastal city is captured in Norfolk, where a rich maritime history coexists peacefully with a diverse population and a thriving city center. Explore Norfolk's historic ports, immerse yourself in its art and culture, or indulge in waterfront cuisine for a vibrant and stimulating experience that captures the city's distinct personality and charm.

Richmond: The Capital of the Old Dominion

Richmond, located in Virginia along the James River, is the Old Dominion's imposing capital. The city provides a remarkable mix of traditional and contemporary because of its extensive history, stunning architecture, and vibrant cultural scene. Here is a thorough examination of Richmond and the activities it provides, highlighting its position as the social, political, and commercial center of Virginia:

Historical Sites:

- Explore the city's historic sites first, starting with the Virginia State Capitol. This famous neoclassical structure, designed by Thomas Jefferson, is not only a working government building but also a reminder of the state's lengthy history.

- Visit the venerable St. John's Church, the location of Patrick Henry's infamous "Give me liberty or give me death" speech during the American Revolution. Immerse yourself in the revolutionary fervor that characterized the nation's founding.

- Discover the sculptures honoring notable Virginians from the past, including Robert E. Lee and Arthur Ashe, along Historic Monument Avenue. Admire the impressive architecture and boulevards studded with trees that make this route a national treasure.

Culture and Museums Institutions:

- Richmond is home to a wide variety of museums and cultural centers that explore different facets of the city's history and artistic culture.

- One of the biggest and most extensive art museums in the country is the Virginia Museum of Fine Arts. Its vast collection contains creations by well-known artists from throughout the world that date back thousands of years.

- Visit the American Civil War Museum to learn more about Richmond's crucial contribution to the Civil War. Learn about the city's importance as the Confederate capital and its effect on the result of the war via interactive displays and relics.

- Discover the Virginia Black History Museum and Cultural Center, which is devoted to promoting and conserving the contributions made by African Americans to the history and culture of Richmond.

Outdoor Recreation along the Riverfront:

- The James River's proximity to Richmond provides many options for outdoor leisure and visual splendor.

- Visit the picturesque Canal Walk, a waterfront promenade that displays the city's industrial past and provides breathtaking views of the river and its environs, and go for a walk or a bike ride along it.

- Take a river tour or go kayaking to get a close-up look at the James River, marvel at its rapids, and appreciate the natural settings that have influenced the growth of the city.

- Discover the stunning Maymont Park, a vast urban sanctuary with immaculately kept gardens, a Japanese garden, a kids' farm, and a Victorian home. It's the ideal location for unwinding, enjoying a picnic, or taking a stroll in the outdoors.

Strong Food and Arts Scene:

- Richmond has a strong arts and culinary scene with a wide range of theaters, galleries, and restaurants to check out.

- Visit galleries, and studios, and attend live performances in Richmond's thriving Scott's Addition area, which is home to the arts district.

- Enjoy the gastronomic options of the city, which include a variety of eateries, craft brewers, and food markets that feature the finest in regional and international cuisine.

- Not to be missed is Richmond's thriving First Fridays Art Walk, when galleries open their doors to the public and display the creations of local artists.

Plantations and Old Estates:

- Many beautiful gardens and old estates can be found in Richmond, which gives tourists the chance to go back in time and appreciate how opulent the city once was.

- Visit the Lewis Ginter Botanical Garden to explore a botanical haven with a wide variety of plant collections, themed gardens, and breathtaking scenery. It's a tranquil getaway where you may relax and get in touch with nature.

- Visit Agecroft Hall, a Tudor-style home that was initially constructed in England before being shipped and put back together in Richmond. Visit the estate on a guided tour to discover its intriguing history and take in the lovely grounds that surround it.

The Old Dominion's capital, Richmond, welcomes tourists to immerse themselves in its illustrious past, diverse culture, and lively environment. The city provides a wide variety of activities that perfectly reflect the spirit of Virginia's capital and its ongoing attractiveness, from historic buildings to flourishing arts scenes, outdoor excursions to gastronomic pleasures.

Williamsburg: Traveling Back in Time at Colonial Williamsburg

Williamsburg, a living history museum in Virginia's Historic Triangle, offers visitors a chance to go back in time and live through the colonial period. The city's focal point, Colonial Williamsburg, is a painstakingly preserved and reproduced colonial capital that immerses visitors in the difficulties and everyday routine of America's early inhabitants. Here is a thorough examination of Williamsburg and the adventures it provides, luring you on a trip back in time:

Historic District

- Start your journey by touring Colonial Williamsburg's Historic Area, a painstakingly conserved and restored area of the city.

- Explore the streets that are dotted with taverns, stores, residences, and structures from the colonial period. Engage with historically accurate costumed interpreters who play out historical roles and tell period tales.

- Visit the Governor's Palace, the opulent home of the royal governors of Virginia. Learn about the affluent way of life of the colonial aristocracy as you explore its sumptuous chambers and well-kept grounds.

Crafts and Trades

- Spend time learning about the crafts and trades that were essential to the colonial economy. Visit the many trade shops to see craftsmen doing age-old trades including printing, silversmithing, carpentry, and blacksmithing.

- Ask inquiries, converse with the artisans, and even try out a few of their skills while being guided by their knowledgeable assistance.

Urban Revolution:

- Discover the dramatic events that led up to the American Revolution in Revolutionary City, a daylong interactive experience.

- Watch historical events including Capitol debates, demonstrations against British rule, and interactions between patriots and loyalists be recreated.

- Take part in public debates, converse with the characters, and learn more about historical, political, and ideological issues.

Exhibits and Museums:

- Investigate the many museums and displays in Colonial Williamsburg, which provide a fuller understanding of various facets of colonial life.

- Discover the outstanding collection of fine and decorative arts from the 17th to the early 19th century at the DeWitt Wallace Decorative Arts Museum. Admire the silverware, paintings, pottery, and furniture that display the era's workmanship.

- Visit the museum devoted to American folk art, the Abby Aldrich Rockefeller Folk Art Museum. Admire the beautiful sculptures, textiles, and other original examples of inventiveness.

Historic Plantations and Gardens:

- Wander casually around Colonial Williamsburg's exquisitely designed gardens. Learn about colonial horticulture and the value of gardens in daily life by exploring the Governor's Palace Gardens, the Kitchen Garden, and the Colonial Nursery.

- Explore adjacent historic plantations like the Shirley Plantation or Carter's Grove Plantation by venturing beyond the Historic Area. These exquisite estates provide a window into plantation life and the nuanced history of the area.

Shopping and Dining:

- At the numerous taverns and restaurants in Colonial Williamsburg, indulge in food with a colonial influence. Taste traditional foods like Brunswick stew, seafood prepared in the manner of the colonial era, or substantial meals.

- Look among the stores and boutiques for one-of-a-kind trinkets and handicrafts with a colonial feel. There is something to satisfy every interest, from handcrafted ceramics to historical attire.

Visitors to Colonial Williamsburg may immerse themselves in the sights, sounds, and tales of America's colonial past, on an enthralling trip back in time. Every nook of Williamsburg looks into the hardships, victories, and daily life of the early settlers, from the opulence of the Governor's Palace to the bustling streets populated with craftsmen and historical figures.

Monticello: Thomas Jefferson's Magnificent Estate,

The Monticello estate, which is perched on a picturesque hill in Charlottesville, Virginia, is a tribute to the genius and foresight of Thomas Jefferson, one of the country's founding fathers. This spectacular mansion, which Jefferson himself planned and constructed, is a testament to his inventive architectural style, intellectual curiosity, and close relationship to the earth. This thorough examination of Monticello and the activities it provides invites you to dig into Thomas Jefferson's world:

Home tour

- Start your trip off by taking a tour of Jefferson's home, Monticello, which provides a fascinating look into his life and creative architectural vision.

- Explore the opulent spaces that have been painstakingly renovated to capture the look and feel of Thomas Jefferson's era. Admire the distinctive details, like the octagonal dome, the parlor with its breathtaking vistas, and the personal study where Jefferson pursued his academic interests.

- Learn about Jefferson's many pursuits and innovations, including his obsession with technology and his love of reading and education.

Grounds and Gardens:

- Take a stroll through the carefully kept gardens that encircle Monticello. Discover the peace and beauty of Jefferson's flower gardens, vegetable gardens, and orchards.

- Explore Jefferson's inventive terraced vegetable garden, where he tried crop rotation and introduced new plant species. Learn about his farming methods and his outlook on the value of self-sufficiency.

- Admire the beautiful fusion of nature and architecture as you take in the stunning views of the Virginia countryside from the West Lawn.

The Mulberry Row

- Discover Mulberry Row, a special place that previously housed Monticello's varied workforce, including slaves, talented craftsmen, and servants.

- Learn about the experiences and lives of the residents and employees of Monticello. Learn more about the complicated realities of slavery in Jefferson's day and the impact it had.

- Visit the restored workshops and homes that display the numerous crafts and abilities used by the community of slaves, such as carpentry, blacksmithing, and cooking.

Exhibits and the Visitors Center:

- Start your tour to Monticello in the visitor center where you may immerse yourself in historical context and information about Jefferson's life and accomplishments.

- Learn more about Thomas Jefferson's political career, his contribution to the nation's formation, and his long-lasting influence on American history by exploring interactive exhibits, artifacts, and multimedia presentations.

- Visit the Jefferson Library to browse the selection of books, trinkets, and crafts created in Jefferson's honor.

Special Programs and Events:

- The year-round special activities and programs held at Monticello provide one-of-a-kind chances to interact with Jefferson's world in various ways.

- Attend talks, seminars, and exhibits that examine Jefferson's interests in a variety of fields, including architecture, gardening, and intellectual hobbies.

- Visit living history demonstrations to get a better picture of everyday life at Monticello during Thomas Jefferson's time. Costumed interpreters bring the past to life during these events.

Visitors to Monticello have the opportunity to fully immerse themselves in Thomas Jefferson's world. Monticello provides a multifaceted journey into the life and legacy of one of America's most significant personalities. From the architectural wonder of the mansion to the beauty of the grounds and the tales of the people who lived and worked there.

Fredericksburg: Battlefields and Historic Sites

A city with a rich history and a well-known place in the American Civil War, Fredericksburg is located in Virginia on the banks of the Rappahannock River. Fredericksburg provides a captivating voyage through time, from its well-preserved battlefields to its historic sites. We invite you to learn more about Fredericksburg and the activities it has to offer by providing the following in-depth exploration:

National Military Park at Spotsylvania and Fredericksburg:

- Start your journey of discovery in the huge Fredericksburg and Spotsylvania National Military Park, which protects the locations of several significant Civil War engagements.

- Visit the Fredericksburg Battlefield, the location of the 1862 Battle of Fredericksburg. Learn more about the battle's violent combat by exploring the surroundings and strolling down the "Bloody Lane," a submerged path.

- Continue to the Chancellorsville Battlefield, the scene of another important conflict. Learn about the acts of bravery and clever military planning that influenced the conflict's end.

- Explore more park locations, including the Spotsylvania Court House Battlefield and the Wilderness Battlefield, each with a distinctive history and importance.

The Old Town of Fredericksburg

- Explore the well-preserved 18th and 19th-century buildings and quaint streetscapes of Fredericksburg's historic downtown.

- Explore Market Square, the center of Fredericksburg's social and economic activity since the 18th century, to learn more about the city's rich colonial history. Take in the bustling environment while admiring the antique structures.

- Visit Carl's Ice Cream, a neighborhood landmark that has been dishing out delectable frozen delights since 1947.

Enjoy a scoop of handcrafted ice cream while remembering the tastes of the past.

Historical Sites:

- Several historical sites in Fredericksburg provide insights into the city's history.

- Learn more about the influential Lewis family and their social circle by exploring Kenmore, a grand Georgian estate constructed in the 18th century.

- Visit the Mary Washington House, where George Washington's mother raised her children. Find more about the life of Mary Washington and the influence she had on her well-known son.

- Discover the Rising Sun Tavern, a reconstructed inn from the 18th century where guests and locals gathered for food, drink, and conversation. Experience the aura of colonial-era hospitality by going on a guided tour.

Culture and Museums Institutions :

- Visit the museums and cultural institutes in Fredericksburg to fully experience the city's rich cultural legacy.

- Discover the history and culture of the area via the exhibits and artifacts at the Fredericksburg Area Museum. Discover the history of the city, its role in the Civil War, and the tales of its many ethnic populations.

- Visit the Hugh Mercer Apothecary Shop, a reconstructed pharmacy from the 18th century, to learn about the medicinal procedures used during the period and the difficulties that physicians encountered during the Revolutionary War.

Outdoor Activities:

- Take advantage of Fredericksburg's scenic surroundings and engage in outdoor recreation there.

- Investigate the Rappahannock Canal Path, a beautiful pathway that follows the path of the old canal. Enjoy the views of the river and the surroundings as you stroll or ride a bike along the trail.

- Visit the tranquil Alum Spring Park, a city park featuring a natural spring, strolling paths, and picnic spaces. Enjoy nature's splendor while unwinding in the serene surroundings.

From its key Civil War battlefields to its well-preserved historic sites, Fredericksburg provides a riveting tour through history. Walk in the footsteps of the troops, become lost in history, and learn more about the challenges and sacrifices that built the country.

V. EXPLORING VIRGINIA'S SCENIC MOUNTAINS

Shenandoah National Park: Hiking, Wildlife, and Breathtaking View

Hiking, wildlife, and breathtaking views may be found at Shenandoah National Park.

Shenandoah National Park, which is located in Virginia's magnificent Blue Ridge Mountains, is a paradise for anyone who likes the outdoors and the natural world. The park provides a breathtaking getaway into the wonder of the natural world with its expansive woods, flowing waterfalls, and beautiful landscapes. Here is a thorough examination of Shenandoah National Park and the adventures it provides, luring you to fully appreciate its wonders:

Skyline Drive:

- Start your journey by traveling down Skyline Drive, a picturesque route that winds 105 kilometers into the park's interior. From the several viewpoints along the route, take in the expansive vistas of the Shenandoah Valley and the surrounding mountains.

- As the park displays a kaleidoscope of hues in the autumn and beautiful wildflowers in the spring and summer, take your time to observe the seasons changing.

- A variety of bird species, white-tailed deer, black bears, wild turkeys, and other animals abound in the area; keep a lookout for them.

Hiking Routes

- Get your hiking boots on and scour the vast system of paths that crisscross Shenandoah National Park. There are routes for every level of hiker with over 500 miles in length, ranging from short strolls to strenuous hikes.

- Set out on the well-known Old Rag Mountain climb, a strenuous but rewarding journey that passes through woods and steep scrambles and culminates in breathtaking panoramic vistas.

- Along routes like Dark Hollow Falls, Whiteoak Canyon, and Rose River Falls, you may experience the tranquil beauty of waterfalls. Feel rejuvenated by the air's refreshing spray while listening to the relaxing sounds of flowing water.

Nature and Wildlife:

- Photographers who love the outdoors and animals will find paradise at Shenandoah National Park.

- Discover the Big Meadows, a large, open meadow in the center of the park, where you could see herds of quietly grazing deer or sometimes hear elk bugling.

- Try to identify a variety of bird species, such as warblers, owls, and woodpeckers, by taking a walk along one of the park's numerous paths while birdwatching.

- Learn more about the park's rich flora and animals, as well as its distinct ecosystems and the efforts to maintain them, by participating in ranger-led programs and guided walks.

Picnicking and Camping:

- Spend more time at Shenandoah National Park by tent camping. The park has several campsites with amenities and services for a wonderful camping trip.

- Enjoy a picnic among the park's stunning natural surroundings. There are several picnic spots dotted about, offering a picturesque setting for a leisurely dinner surrounded by the views and sounds of nature.

Ranger Initiatives and Educational Displays:

- Participate in the park rangers' instructional activities and informative displays.

- Learn about the geology, history, and significance of protecting the park's natural resources by attending ranger-led seminars and presentations.

- Take a look at Harry F. Byrd Sr. You may see displays that highlight the park's flora, animals, and cultural legacy at the Visitor Center or the Dickey Ridge Visitor Center.

Shenandoah National Park is a haven of natural beauty that provides a respite from the stress of daily life. Shenandoah National Park is certain to leave you with priceless memories and a profound appreciation for the beauties of the natural world, whether you're seeking adventure on the trails, comfort in the tranquility of nature, or taking breathtaking images.

Charlottesville: A Blend of History, Culture, and Wine

Charlottesville is a bustling city that effortlessly combines a rich history, cultural attractions, and a thriving wine culture. It is located in the Piedmont area of Virginia. Visitors will be captivated by Charlottesville's historical sites, architectural wonders, and vibrant arts and dining communities. Here is a thorough analysis of Charlottesville and the many experiences it provides:

Historical Sites:

- Visit Thomas Jefferson's famous mansion, Monticello, to kick off your tour. Discover the life and legacy of one of America's founding fathers as you tour the perfectly planned residence and grounds.

- Discover the Thomas Jefferson-founded University of Virginia. Investigate the lovely surroundings and the UNESCO World Heritage-listed Academical Village. Admire the Rotunda and the Lawn, two architectural wonders that represent Thomas Jefferson's ideal for education.

Cultural Attractions

- Get lost in Charlottesville's thriving artistic and cultural community.

- Explore the amazing collection of American and European art at the University of Virginia's Fralin Museum of Art. Discover artwork from many eras and genres by exploring the varied exhibits.

- The Paramount Theater, a beautifully renovated historic theater that holds a variety of concerts, plays, and other cultural events, offers live entertainment.

- Explore the Downtown Mall, a boulevard that is welcoming to pedestrians and dotted with boutiques, art galleries, and eateries. Enjoy the live street entertainment, interesting stores, and energetic environment.

<u>Vineyards and Wine</u>:

- Charlottesville is located in the center of Virginia's wine region, providing the ideal setting for vineyard excursions and wine tastings.

- Visit some of the area's well-known vineyards, including King Family Vineyards, Jefferson Vineyards, and Barboursville Vineyards. While admiring the stunning vineyard surroundings, sample a range of wines, from crisp whites to strong reds.

- Take a leisurely drive through the area's vineyards and rolling hills along the Monticello Wine Trail. Discover the many vineyards in Virginia and enjoy the tastes they have to offer.

Gastronomic Delights

- The food scene in Charlottesville is a fascinating mix of farm-to-table fare, world tastes, and regional specialties.

- Find fresh fruit, handmade items, and mouth watering delicacies in the city's local food markets, including the City Market and the Farmers Market.

- Dine at one of the numerous award-winning establishments that highlight the best ingredients and culinary innovation in the area. Charlottesville has a variety of eating facilities to suit every taste, from cutting-edge farm-to-table restaurants to warm Southern cafes.

Outdoor Activities:

- There are many chances for outdoor leisure in the area around Charlottesville for nature lovers.

- Discover the trails of the nearby Shenandoah National Park, which offers hiking, picnicking, and animal viewing possibilities along with breathtaking vistas and cascading waterfalls.

- Take a leisurely drive along the Blue Ridge Parkway, which is well-known for its panoramic views and charming overlooks. As you travel along this gorgeous byway, take in the grandeur of the nearby mountains and valleys.

You are invited to experience Charlottesville's rich history, thriving culture, and the aromas of Virginia's wine region. Charlottesville provides a wide variety of activities that will leave you with treasured memories of your trip to this charming city, from historical buildings and top-notch museums to culinary pleasures and natural beauty.

Roanoke: The Blue Ridge Mountains' Entryway

Roanoke, located in the magnificent Blue Ridge Mountains of Virginia, is a charming entryway to the region's natural splendor, outdoor activities, and cultural experiences. Roanoke provides a great combination of urban comforts and outdoor adventure thanks to its historic history, thriving arts scene, and proximity to stunning vistas.

Here is a thorough analysis of Roanoke and the many sensations it provides:

The Old Town of Roanoke:

- Start your adventure in Roanoke's historic downtown, where you can discover the lively culture and rich history of the area.

- Take a stroll around the city's busy center, Market Square, and take in the vibrant atmosphere. Visit regional art galleries, interesting stores, and historical architecture.

- Discover the Taubman Museum of Art, which features a varied collection of creations by local and international artists. Explore the realm of contemporary art and marvel at the thought-provoking exhibits.

Highway to Blue Ridge:

- Take a picturesque trip through America's Blue Ridge Parkway, one of the country's most beautiful roads. The perfect place to begin this magnificent tour is in Roanoke.

- As you drive through the Blue Ridge Mountains, take in the expansive views and several chances to pause at overlooks to admire the majesty of the surroundings.

- Discover the mountain hiking routes that wind across the landscape, providing opportunities to see breathtaking landscapes, flowing waterfalls, and a variety of species.

Outdoor Activities:

- With its abundance of leisure options, Roanoke is a paradise for those who like the great outdoors.

- Take a hike to the famous McAfee Knob, one of the Appalachian Trail's most popular picture locations. Enjoy panoramic vistas of the valley below and create priceless memories with the mountains as a background.

- Explore Park, which is located along the banks of the Roanoke River, and take in its serene beauty. This beautiful park has hiking and bike routes, picnic sites, and canoeing and fishing options.

Cultural Encounters:

- Take part in the rich arts and cultural scene of Roanoke.

- Visit the Roanoke Pinball Museum to play a selection of antique pinball machines and learn about the development of this well-known game.

- Discover the Center in the Square, a cultural complex with galleries, performing venues, and museums. Learn about the Roanoke Symphony Orchestra, the Harrison Museum of African American Culture, and the Science Museum of Western Virginia.

Local Food and Beer

- Discover Roanoke's food culture and craft breweries to indulge in its tastes.

- At the city's farm-to-table eateries, savor delicious meals made with regional products. Roanoke provides a variety of gastronomic experiences, from foreign cuisine to comfort food from the South.

- Visit the neighborhood breweries and brewpubs to learn more about the city's craft beer sector. Discover the skill of creating beer, meet the brewers, and sample a range of artisan beers.

The Blue Ridge Mountains' spectacular scenery and outdoor experiences may be reached through the alluring gateway city of Roanoke. Roanoke provides a lovely fusion of metropolitan conveniences and unspoiled natural beauty that is guaranteed to make an impact, whether you're looking for cultural adventures, outdoor exploration, or just a peaceful vacation in nature.

Natural Bridge: Nature's Spectacle in the Appalachian Mountains

Natural Bridge, which is situated in Virginia's picturesque Appalachian Mountains, is a wonderful example of the strength and magnificence of nature. This natural marvel, which took millions of years to form, mesmerizes tourists with its magnificent arch, breathtaking surroundings, and extensive geological past.

Here is an in-depth analysis of Natural Bridge and the breathtaking experiences it provides:

The Natural Bridge

- Admire the Natural Bridge, which is the primary draw. This impressive 215-foot-long, 66-foot-tall limestone arch creates an amazing sight. You will be in awe of this natural beauty when you look up at it and appreciate the forces that have molded the terrain over millennia.

- The Cedar Creek Trail, which runs underneath the bridge and offers interesting vistas and up-close views of the arch, is a great place to take a stroll. Take pictures to capture this amazing geological formation's memories.

Natural Bridge State Park

- Discover the region around the Natural Bridge at Natural Bridge State Park. Participate in a variety of leisure pursuits while taking in the park's breathtaking scenery.

- Hike along one of the park's many paths, which weave through luxuriant woods, along to the peaceful Cedar Creek, and provide sweeping views of the surrounding mountains.

- Learn about the history, culture, and customs of the Monacan Native American tribe at the Monacan Indian Living History Exhibit. Gain an understanding of their way of life and learn about their strong connection to the earth.

Lost River and Lace Falls:

- Explore further local natural beauties by going beyond the Natural Bridge.

- Check out Lace Falls, a lovely waterfall that cascades down several rock formations. Enjoy the peace of the area for a bit and listen to the relaxing sound of the river flowing.

- Learn about the underground river called Lost River, which runs through caverns. Explore the secret corridors on a guided tour and be amazed by the subterranean marvels the erosive force of water has wrought.

Natural Bridge Caverns:

- Visit the Natural Bridge Caverns, which are close to the Natural Bridge, to delve into the earth's interior.

- Enter the subterranean world and explore the fascinating stalactites and stalagmites rock formations. During the caves' guided tours, you may discover more about the geological processes that formed these distinctive features.

- Discover the magnificent Cathedral Room, the system's biggest chamber, where you'll be surrounded by stunning natural formations that exude a feeling of majesty.

Outdoor Activities and Picnics:

- Participate in outdoor activities while admiring the nearby Appalachian Mountains' natural splendor.

- Use the picnic spots at Natural Bridge State Park to have a leisurely dinner while surrounded by the beauty of nature.

- Take a walk around the beautiful scenery, go birding, explore the local hiking and bike trails, or just relax.

- Natural Bridge is a tribute to the strength and magnificence of nature, encouraging people to experience its majesty and immerse themselves in the alluring landscapes of the Appalachian Mountains. Natural Bridge is an amazing experience that will leave you with a profound appreciation for the marvels of the natural world, whether you're admiring the magnificent arch, exploring the state park and its trails, or going into the depths of the caves.

VI. IMMERSE YOURSELF IN VIRGINIA'S CULTURE

Museums and Art Galleries: Showcasing Virginia's Rich Heritage

The history and culture of Virginia are intricately entwined with those of the rest of the United States. Virginia has contributed significantly to the development of the United States, from its colonial roots through key turning points in the country's history.

By presenting artifacts, works of art, and exhibitions that showcase Virginia's past, museums and art galleries all around the state provide an insight into this fascinating history. The following renowned museums and art galleries enable visitors to fully experience Virginia's rich past:

Virginia Museum of Fine Arts:

- A world-class museum that holds a vast collection of works of art from over 5,000 years of human history is the Virginia Museum of Fine Arts.

- Discover the different exhibits in the museum's galleries, which include pieces from classical antiquity, ancient Egypt, European masters, American art, and contemporary artists.

- Admire classic works like Edgar Degas' sculpture "Little Dancer Aged Fourteen" and Gilbert Stuart's painting of George Washington.

Jamestown Settlement (Williamsburg):

- Explore the history of the first permanent English colony in America at the Jamestown colony, a living history museum.

- Through interactive displays, replica homes, and historically accurate costumed interpreters, you can experience life in 17th-century Virginia.

- Find more about the early immigrants' hardships and successes, their connections with Native American tribes, and the founding of the Jamestown colony.

Virginia Museum of History & Culture

- The rich history of Virginia is committed to being preserved and presented through the Virginia Museum of History & Culture.

- Discover interesting exhibitions that explore a range of historical topics, such as the American Revolution, the Civil War, African American history, and more, with Virginia.

- View historical items including Civil War uniforms, Native American relics, and papers that notable Virginians like Thomas Jefferson and George Washington have signed.

Colonial Williamsburg:

- At Colonial Williamsburg, a living history museum and outdoor architectural museum that recreates the Virginian state capital of the 18th century goes back in time.

- Explore the painstakingly rebuilt structures, engage with the costumed interpreters, and discover what it was like to live, vote, and practice politics in colonial Virginia.

- Explore the impressive collection of American folk art, including paintings, furniture, and decorative arts, at the

Abby Aldrich Rockefeller Folk Art Museum.

Virginia Aviation Museum:

- The Virginia Aviation Museum, which is devoted to preserving and displaying Virginia's aviation heritage, is open to visitors who are interested in flying.

- A collection of historic aircraft, including military planes, helicopters, and even a copy of the Wright Brothers' 1903 Flyer, may be found here.

- Find more about Virginia's contributions to the history of aviation, such as its illustrious pilots and ground-breaking aircraft designs.

Chrysler Museum of Art

- The Chrysler Museum of Art, which is situated in Norfolk, is well known for its extensive collection of works of art that date back thousands of years.

- View the exhibits at the museum's galleries, which include American paintings, modern pieces, glass art, and more.

- Enjoy the works of art by Rembrandt, Monet, Picasso, and Warhol.

These are just a handful of the many museums and art galleries that highlight Virginia's extensive cultural legacy. If you're interested in fine art, colonial history, aviation, or the state's overall history, Virginia's cultural institutions provide a plethora of exhibitions and collections that may help you learn more about the past of the area and how it affected the rest of the country.

Festivals and Music: Celebrating the Vibrant Arts Scene

There is a thriving arts scene in Virginia that includes a variety of musical genres and cultural manifestations. The state provides a wide range of musical experiences to suit all interests, from classical symphonies to contemporary music festivals. Numerous festivals also honor the arts, highlighting regional talent and drawing well-known performers from all over the globe. The following Virginia music venues and events deserve special mention:

<u>Wolf Trap National Park for the Performing Arts:</u>

- Just outside of Washington, D.CThere is a unique national park called Wolf

Trap that is devoted to the performing arts.

- At the Filene Center, an outdoor amphitheater tucked away in a beautiful natural environment, take in acts of the highest caliber.

- Discover a range of musical styles, such as jazz, pop, rock, and more. Theater shows and dance events are frequently held in the park.

The Virginia Opera (several locations)

- Virginia Opera is famous for its outstanding presentations, which include both traditional and modern opera.

- A number of the state's cities, including Richmond, Norfolk, and Fairfax, host performances.

- Enjoy this renowned opera company's dramatic storyline, alluring songs, and breathtaking performances.

Richmond Folk Festival

- The Richmond Folk Festival is a yearly celebration of the variety of traditional music and culture that is eagerly anticipated.

- Three days of live performances by famous folk artists from various musical traditions from across the globe are available for your enjoyment.

- Discover interactive exhibitions, food stands, and artisan demonstrations that celebrate the many communities' rich cultural history.

FloydFest:

- FloydFest is a multi-day music and art event hosted in Virginia's picturesque Blue Ridge Mountains.

- You may listen to a combination of Americana, folk, bluegrass, rock, and world music.

- Take in concerts by both well-known and up-and-coming artists on several stages, as well as art exhibitions, workshops, and outdoor activities.

Festival of Lockn' (Arrington):

- A four-day music event called Lockn' event honors a variety of musical styles, from rock and blues to funk and jam bands.

- The event is held at Infinity Downs Farm in Arrington, Virginia, providing music lovers with a gorgeous location.

- Discover original collaborations, longer sets, and unforgettable performances by prominent artists in a lively festival setting.

The Norfolk-based NorVa

- The NorVa is a storied music venue in Norfolk that is well-known for showcasing live performances by performers from all over the world and from different genres.

- The NorVa provides an intimate venue for outstanding events, with everything from rock and alternative to hip-hop and electronic music.

These music venues and events are but a sample of Virginia's thriving arts community. Numerous concerts, shows, and cultural events are held all around the state each year to showcase the skills of regional artists and draw in international artists. All music enthusiasts may have a vibrant and educational experience in Virginia's music and festival scene, regardless of their preference for classical music, folk music, or modern genres.

VII. OUTDOOR ADVENTURES IN VIRGINIA

Water Sports: Kayaking, Canoeing, and Beach Excursions

Virginia is a haven for water aficionados because of its wealth of waterways, which include rivers, lakes, and a breathtaking coastline. Virginia has a wide selection of water activities that are suitable for people of all skill levels, whether you're looking for exhilarating experiences or peaceful moments on the water. Here are some thrilling water sports you may enjoy in Virginia:

<u>Canoeing and kayaking:</u>

- Take a kayaking or canoeing trip along one of Virginia's beautiful rivers, such as the Shenandoah, Rappahannock, or James.

- Explore moderate rapids, float along tranquil waterways, and take in the beauty of nature all around you.

- Watch out for animals such as herons, turtles, and possibly bald eagles along the riverbanks.

SUP: Stand-Up Paddleboarding

- On the calm waters of Virginia's lakes and reservoirs, like Smith Mountain Lake or Lake Anna, try your hand at stand-up paddling.

- Enjoy a unique viewpoint as you float across the water while standing on a paddleboard and using the paddle to go ahead.

- Enjoy the sunshine, practice your balance, and take in the serenity of your surroundings.

Virginia Norfolk

- Visit Virginia Beach, a well-known seaside location, and partake in several water sports.

- Build sandcastles, relax, and take in the sun while relaxing on the sandy shoreline.

- Try surfing, swimming in the roiling waves, or taking a bath in the Atlantic Ocean.

- In the crystal-clear seas off the shore, enjoy snorkeling or scuba diving to discover the diverse marine life.

Whale and Dolphin Watching:

- For a genuinely unique experience, go on a dolphin or whale-watching excursion along Virginia's coast.

- Observe these gorgeous animals as they swim and play in the water, in their natural environment.

- On the boat, you'll be accompanied by professional instructors who can teach you about their behavior and conservation initiatives.

Chincoteague and Assateague Islands:

- Visit the islands of Assateague and Chincoteague, known for their distinctive fauna and gorgeous beaches.

- Renting a kayak or canoe will enable you to explore the calm waters around the islands and get up close to the varied coastal ecology.

- Admire the renowned wild ponies that wander uninhibitedly on Assateague

Island—a breathtaking and alluring sight.

Lake Anna State Park:

- At Spotsylvania County's Lake Anna State Park, spend the day engaging in water-related activities.

- Rent a kayak, canoe, or paddleboat to explore the lake's tranquil waters.

- Go bass, catfish, or sunfish fishing, or just unwind on the sandy beach and cool off in the water.

Virginia provides a wide variety of water sports to suit every choice, whether you like the exhilaration of kayaking through rapids, the tranquility of paddling on a tranquil lake, or the leisure of seaside experiences. So gather your supplies, enjoy the water, and immerse yourself in Virginia's aquatic beauties to make lifelong memories.

Hiking and Camping: Exploring Virginia's Trails and Campgrounds

With its numerous landscapes, which vary from coastal plains to rolling hills and beautiful mountains, Virginia is a sanctuary for outdoor lovers. The state provides many options for hiking and camping trips because of its wide route system and plenty of well-equipped campsites. Here are some outstanding hiking routes and campsites to discover in Virginia, regardless of your level of experience backpacking or your level of casual nature appreciation:

Appalachian Trail

- Take a hike along a section of the fabled Appalachian Trail, which winds for more than 550 miles across Virginia.

- As you travel along this renowned path, you will see stunning panoramas, pass through dense woods, and overcome strenuous terrain.

- McAfee Knob, Dragon's Tooth, and the Grayson Highlands—where you may see wild ponies—are notable areas.

Shenandoah National Park

- With more than 500 miles of hiking trails, Shenandoah National Park is a natural wonderland.

- The Skyline Drive, a picturesque road that snakes through the park and offers several trailheads and stunning overlooks, is the most well-known route through the area.

- Discover the splendor of the park by hiking on well-known trails including

Old Rag Mountain, Whiteoak Canyon, and Dark Hollow Falls.

George Washington and Jefferson National Forests:

- Over one million acres of hiking and camping options may be found in the George Washington and Jefferson National Forests.

- Explore a variety of environments, such as ancient forests, gushing waterfalls, and lovely meadows.

- The Devil's Marbleyard, McAfee's Knob, and Crabtree Falls are a few well-liked paths that provide various topographies and degrees of difficulty.

Grayson Highlands Park:

- Visit Grayson Highlands State Park in southwest Virginia, which is renowned for its wild horses and untamed beauty.

- Discover the routes that wind past rocky outcrops, tranquil woodlands, and alpine meadows while providing sweeping vistas of the neighboring mountains.

- Make sure to climb Mount Rogers National Recreation Area, Virginia's highest mountain, to see the magnificent wild ponies that live there.

Assateague Island National Seashore:

- Off Virginia's eastern coast, on Assateague Island, you may go camping and hiking along the seashore.

- Discover sand pathways that meander through dunes, marshes, and beachside settings, letting you take in the natural beauty of the island.

- Set a tent close to the shore, take in the sound of the pounding waves, and try to find the renowned wild ponies that roam the island freely.

Campgrounds:

- Several campsites in Virginia may accommodate different camping needs.

- Shenandoah River State Park, Pocahontas State Park, and Chippokes Plantation State Park are a few well-known campgrounds that include picturesque campsites and amenities including hiking paths, fishing holes, and picnic spaces.

- Private campsites and RV parks are also spread out over the state, adding more possibilities for camping and outdoor activities.

Keep in mind to follow park restrictions, respect the environment, and follow Leave No Trace principles while exploring Virginia's trails and campsites. Virginia's hiking trails and campsites provide an exceptional outdoor experience for all nature lovers, whether they are looking for alone time in the woods, spectacular views, or just the simple delight of being in nature.

Biking and Other Sports: Outdoor thrills in Virginia's Great Outdoors

Biking and participating in other outdoor activities are abundant in Virginia, which is a haven for fans of outdoor sports. The state offers bikers of all skill levels everything from picturesque road routes to heart-pounding mountain terrain. Additionally, Virginia's varied landscapes provide a setting for a variety of outdoor sports and leisure pursuits. Here are some exhilarating outdoor activities and riding routes in Virginia:

Virginia Capital Trail:

- The 52-mile paved Virginia Capital Trail links Richmond and Jamestown and allows visitors to take in both the natural beauty and historical significance of the state.

- Take a leisurely ride across the beautiful countryside, passing past historic sites, plantations, and quaint little villages.

- For bikers of all ages and skill levels, the path provides a beautiful and secure route.

Shenandoah Valley

- Discover the beautiful Shenandoah Valley's many bike possibilities.

- Take a lovely ride along the Valley Pike Bicycle Route, which passes past wineries, quaint villages, and open fields.

- Massanutten Resort near McGaheysville provides a network of thrilling trails for mountain bikers, including downhill runs and challenging singletracks.

Virginia Creeper Trail:

- Start a fascinating bicycle journey along the 34-mile Virginia Creeper Trail, which meanders through the Blue Ridge Mountains' breathtaking scenery.

- The path travels through woods, meadows, and stunning trestles while alternating between easy-riding and exhilarating downhill parts.

- Take a leisurely ride while admiring the gorgeous scenery and the odd animal sighting by renting a bike or bringing your own.

Rock Climbing:

- Numerous rock climbing locations in Virginia are open to climbers of all abilities.

- A well-known climbing site with a range of routes for climbers of all levels is the New River Gorge, which is situated in southern West Virginia close to the Virginia border.

- Seneca Rocks, Old Rag Mountain, and McAfee Knob are three further well-liked climbing locations that each provide distinctive rock formations and thrilling climbs.

Water Sports

- Enjoy exhilarating water activities like kayaking, canoeing, paddleboarding, and whitewater rafting by taking advantage of Virginia's rivers.

- For those who like water activities, the James River, Rappahannock River, and New River provide fantastic options.

- For sports like jet skiing, water skiing, and wakeboarding, you may also explore reservoirs and lakes like Smith Mountain Lake or Lake Anna.

Disc Golf

- Disc golf fans may test their abilities on a variety of courses in Virginia.

- Investigate venues like Blockhouse Disc Golf and Country Club in Spotsylvania County, New Quarter Park in York County, and Hawk Hollow in Spotsylvania County.

- Aim for the baskets and put your disc golf skills to the test while taking in the beautiful surroundings.

No matter whether you like water sports, rock climbing, or cycling, Virginia's beautiful outdoors provides many opportunities for exhilarating excursions and life-changing encounters.

VIII. HIDDEN GEMS AND DAY TRIP

OFF THE BEATEN PATH: VIRGINIA'S LESSER-KNOWN TREASURES

Virginia is well known for its historical landmarks, bustling towns, and breathtaking natural marvels, but the state also has several undiscovered jewels that provide distinctive and off-the-beaten-path experiences. These lesser-known gems provide surprising glimpses into Virginia's rich history, varied cultures, and breathtaking scenery. Here are some Virginia hidden treasures worth seeing if you want to go beyond the well-known tourist spots:

<u>Tangier Island:</u>

- Escape to the secluded island of Tangier Island in the Chesapeake Bay.

- Explore this little fishing town, renowned for its unique accent and picturesque environment, and take a trip back in time.

- Learn about the history of the island, go to the Tangier History Museum, and enjoy fresh seafood in neighborhood restaurants.

Natural Tunnels State Park:

- Visit Natural Tunnel State Park in Duffield, which is home to a geological marvel referred to as the "Eighth Wonder of the World."

- Discover the hiking routes that lead to the 10-story-high natural tunnel, which was created when a river dug through a limestone ridge.

- Enjoy sweeping views of the surrounding mountains and the

spectacular tunnel below by riding a picturesque chairlift.

Abingdon:

- Visit the quaint village of Abingdon, which is hidden in Virginia's southwest.

- Wander around the historic area, which is dotted with bustling stores and wonderfully restored 19th-century structures.

- Watch a performance at the famed Barter Theater, one of the country's oldest professional resident theaters.

Cape Charles

- On Virginia's Eastern Shore, explore the seaside community of Cape Charles.

- Take in the small-town ambiance, wander through the charming neighborhoods, and relax on the spotless beach.

- Discover the history and maritime legacy of the town by visiting the Cape Charles Museum.

Devil's Bathtub:

- In Scott County, look for Devil's Bathtub, a buried treasure.

- Set off on a leisurely trek through verdant trees and across a brook to reach a natural pool with blue-green water that is stunningly clean.

- Swim in the cool water or just take in the beauty of this remote location.

Wise County:

- Explore the Appalachian culture and natural beauty of Wise County in southwest Virginia.

- Visit Breaks Interstate Park, frequently referred to as the "Grand Canyon of the South," which offers amazing vistas and beautiful canyons.

- Visit the Southwest Virginia Museum Historical State Park to learn more about the history and customs of the area.

These lesser-known Virginia gems provide interested visitors with a peek at the state's undiscovered attractions and offer unique experiences. These off-the-beaten-path locations exhibit Virginia's rich legacy and provide the chance to make unforgettable experiences, whether you're looking for isolated natural sites, beautiful tiny towns, or cultural jewels

Day Trips from Major Cities: Touring the Regions Around Virginia

The state's biggest cities function as entryways to its varied topography, historical landmarks, and cultural attractions. Even while each city offers a lot to see, day excursions to the surrounding countryside let you experience even more of Virginia's beauty and charm. Following are some tempting day travel ideas from Virginia's largest cities:

Exploring Richmond:

- Colonial Williamsburg: Visit Colonial Williamsburg to go back in time to the 18th century. Discover America's colonial history by strolling through the historic neighborhoods and interacting with costumed interpreters.

- Experience the Lewis Ginter Botanical Garden's spectacular gardens, plant collections, and picturesque settings to fully appreciate nature's splendor.

- Escape to Belle Isle, a peaceful natural haven in the James River. Enjoy the chance to put your toes in the river, the beautiful scenery, and the hiking paths.

In Norfolk:

- Indulge in water activities like surfing, paddle boarding, or jet skiing at the adjacent Virginia Beach, where you can enjoy the sun on its gorgeous beaches, stroll along the famous boardwalk, and more.

- Experience the 23-mile-long bridge that connects the Eastern Shore to the mainland, the Chesapeake Bay Bridge Tunnel, an engineering wonder. Enjoy the opportunity to see dolphins and amazing scenery.

- Visit the historic Cape Henry Lighthouse, which is situated near the mouth of the Chesapeake Bay. To get a panoramic picture of the coastline, climb to the summit.

In Roanoke:

- Blue Ridge Parkway: Take a gorgeous drive along this breathtaking route that snakes through the Blue Ridge Mountains, the Blue Ridge Parkway. Enjoy breathtaking views, hiking routes, and chances to see animals.

- Explore the Virginia Tech Campus: Travel a short distance to Blacksburg to see the university's stunning campus. Visit the Hahn Horticulture Garden, the Moss Arts Center, or Lane Stadium to see a sporting event.

- Natural Bridge: Explore the Natural Bridge, a Cedar Creek-spanning geological wonder. Discover the nearby trails and take in the magnificence of this natural monument.

Charlottesville

- Take a picturesque journey along the Monticello Wine Trail to learn more about Virginia's wine region. Visit wineries, take part in tastings, and explore the area's stunning vineyards.

- Visit Shenandoah National Park to take advantage of the hiking trails, flowing waterfalls, and breathtaking views along Skyline Drive. Don't overlook well-known vantage locations like Hawksbill Summit or Stony Man.

- University of Virginia: Take a day to see the university's iconic campus, which Thomas Jefferson designed. Explore the Rotunda, take a walk around the lovely grounds, and take in the college ambiance.

Alexandria:

- Mount Vernon: Visit George Washington's historic home, Mount Vernon. Learn about the life and legacy of America's first president as you tour the home and meander around the grounds.

- Explore the quaint alleys of Old Town Fredericksburg, which is renowned for its restored historic neighborhood. Visit historic sites including the

Fredericksburg Battlefield and small boutiques and art galleries.

- George Washington's Distillery & Gristmill: Go to Mount Vernon to see George Washington's Distillery & Gristmill. Discover how whiskey is made while seeing examples of milling methods used in the 18th century.

These days, excursions provide a range of experiences, from historical immersion to natural beauty and cultural discovery, all from Virginia's main cities. These days, excursions enable you to maximize your time in Virginia and build lifelong experiences, whether your interests are in history, outdoor activities, or just exploring the region.

IX. PRACTICAL INFORMATION AND TIPS

Getting Around

To assist you in navigating the state and taking in its many attractions, Virginia provides a variety of transportation alternatives. There are choices to fit your travel tastes, whether you like the comfort of driving, the effectiveness of public transit, or the gorgeous paths of cycling. The following are some popular ways to navigate Virginia:

Auto Rentals

- With the freedom and convenience of a rental automobile, you can explore Virginia at your leisure.

- Several automobile rental companies in Virginia's major towns and airports provide a variety of vehicles to suit your requirements.

- Plan your routes appropriately and keep an eye out for any road closures or construction, keeping in mind that traffic in metropolitan areas might be crowded.

Using Public Transit:

- Commuter train service is provided by Virginia Railway Express (VRE), which mainly serves northern Virginia and Washington, D.C. urban settings .

- If you're traveling to Washington, D.C., use the Washington Metropolitan Area Transit Authority (WMATA). WMATA runs an extensive Metrorail and Metrobus network across the metropolitan region.

- In the Hampton Roads area, which includes Norfolk and Virginia Beach, Hampton Roads Transit (HRT) offers bus, light rail, and ferry services.

- The bus services in the Richmond metropolitan region are run by the Greater Richmond Transit Company (GRTC).

Amtrak:

- Amtrak provides rail connections to Virginia's largest cities, including Charlottesville, Richmond, Norfolk, and Alexandria.

- The Carolinian/Piedmont and Northeast Regional lines provide simple connections to other East Coast locations.

Cycling:

- You may travel Virginia's beautiful roadways and bike paths to discover the state's natural splendor.

- Numerous communities, including Richmond, Norfolk, and Alexandria, have bike-sharing programs that provide a cheap and environmentally beneficial choice for local short journeys.

- Cycling enthusiasts enjoy the 52-mile, paved Virginia Capital Trail, which connects Richmond and Jamestown.

Flights

- Norfolk International Airport (ORF), Washington Dulles International Airport (IAD), and Ronald Reagan Washington National Airport (DCA) are just a few of the airports that serve Virginia.

- There are both domestic and international planes accessible, making it simple to travel to Virginia's many locations.

Ridesharing and Local Taxis:

- In Virginia's biggest cities, taxis and ridesharing services like Uber and Lyft are easily accessible.

- For quick excursions inside cities or for getting to and from airports or railway terminals, they provide a practical choice.

- Take into account variables like traffic, parking, and distances between locations as you plan your route throughout Virginia. To ensure pleasant and effective travel, it is always a good idea to check for any transit changes or timetables in advance.

Accommodation Option in Virginia

Virginia has a wide variety of lodging options to meet the needs and budgets of every tourist. You'll discover a range of alternatives around the state, whether you're seeking opulent hotels, quaint bed & breakfasts, snug cabins, or affordable options. Here are some well-known locations and neighborhoods in Virginia where you may locate lodging:

Regions around Virginia

- **Arlington**: Arlington, which is only on the other side of the Potomac River from Washington, D.C., has a variety of hotels that are suitable for both business and pleasure guests. It serves as an ideal starting point for touring the capital area.

- Alexandria, a city renowned for its ancient beauty, offers boutique hotels and bed & breakfasts housed in beautifully maintained structures. The city offers a distinctive fusion of history and contemporary conveniences and gives simple access to Washington, D.C.

Central and Richmond, Virginia

- Downtown Richmond: The center of the capital city is home to a range of hotels, from five-star resorts to modest inns. Staying near the city center makes it simple to see landmarks like the Virginia State Capitol, museums, and the thriving eating scene.

- Charlottesville: Charlottesville, the city where the University of Virginia is located, has a variety of hotels, inns, and bed & breakfasts. The city's historic attractions, vineyards, and the surrounding Shenandoah National Park may all be explored from here.

Coastal Virginia and Hampton Roads:

- Virginia Beach: As a well-liked beach resort, Virginia Beach has a variety of lodging options, such as hotels, resorts, and rental homes along the coast. The region is well-known for its lovely sandy beaches and bustling beachfront.

- Hotels may be found in Norfolk's downtown and waterfront, giving visitors quick access to places like the Battleship Wisconsin, Nauticus Maritime Museum, and Chrysler Museum of Art.

Mountains in the Blue Ridge and Shenandoah valleys:

- For visitors wishing to experience the picturesque splendor and hiking trails of Shenandoah National Park, Front Royal, which is close to the park's entrance, provides hotels, motels, and cottages.

- Staunton: This city, well-known for its Blackfriars Playhouse and historic downtown, offers attractive bed & breakfasts and boutique hotels that let guests fully experience the city's rich cultural legacy.

Western Virginia:

From resorts along the Blue Ridge Parkway to motels in the downtown area, Roanoke provides a range of lodging options. It acts as a point of entry to the region's breathtaking natural settings, such as the

Appalachian Trail and the Blue Ridge Mountains.

Eastern Coast:

- Cape Charles offers a variety of bed & breakfasts, inns, and vacation accommodations. It is a quaint seaside hamlet on Maryland's Eastern Shore. It's the perfect location for anybody looking for a tranquil beach escape.

- Consider the location of your planned activities, the facilities you want, and the ambiance that meets your tastes when deciding where to stay in Virginia. It's a good idea to reserve lodging in advance to assure availability and lock in the best deals, particularly during busy travel times.

Safety Tips and Helpful Contacts

Although it's normally safe to go to Virginia, it's always wise to put your safety first and be ready. Following are some safety recommendations and crucial phone numbers to keep in mind when visiting:

Tips for general safety

- Be mindful of your surroundings and believe in your gut. It's wise to leave if you feel uneasy in a place or circumstance.

- Keep your valuables hidden and safe, particularly in busy locations and popular tourist destinations.

- When you're not there, lock the doors and windows of your hotel room and automobile.

- Keep yourself hydrated, particularly during the hot summer months, and avoid sunburn by applying sunscreen and wearing the proper attire.

- When taking part in outdoor activities, such as hiking, swimming, or boating, heed all safety recommendations and cautions.

Emergency numbers:

Emergency Services: In the event of an emergency, such as a medical emergency, an accident, or a crime, dial 911 for urgent help. Non-Emergency Police: Get in touch with your neighborhood's police department if you need help in a non-emergency scenario. Medical Resources:

X. IDEAL TRAVEL ITINERARY

First day: Getting to Richmond

- Discover Richmond's downtown, featuring Shockoe Slip and the Virginia State Capitol.

- Visit Maymont, a lovely estate with gardens and animal displays, as well as the Virginia Museum of Fine Arts.

- Visit a famous restaurant in Richmond for a delectable meal.

Second day: Old Charlottesville

- Travel to Charlottesville and see Thomas Jefferson's stunning mansion, Monticello.

- Explore the Rotunda and Lawn as well as the University of Virginia's historic campus.

- Discover the dynamic local cuisine and craft beverage scene in Charlottesville's central business district.

Day 3: Shenandoah National Park

- Drive the beautiful Skyline Drive to Shenandoah National Park.

- Enjoy the chance to see animals, stunning views, and hiking routes.

- Enjoy a picnic at the park while admiring the Blue Ridge Mountains breathtaking scenery.

Day 4: Coastal Virginia

- Take a trip to Virginia Beach and spend the day lounging on the stunning beaches.

- Investigate the lively boardwalk area when visiting the Virginia Aquarium & Marine Science Center.

- Enjoy a supper of delicious seafood while taking in the coastal ambiance.

Day 5: Old Williamsburg

- Drive to historic Williamsburg to experience the historic ambiance of the 18th century.

- Visit living history museums and take part in interactive historical recreations.

- Enjoy the Dining selections while taking a stroll around Merchants Square's charming streets.

Day 6: Adorable Norfolk

- The USS Wisconsin and the Nauticus Nautical Museum are great places to learn about Norfolk's nautical history.

- Explore the Chrysler Museum of Art and take a walk along Norfolk's lovely shoreline.

- Experience the vibrant arts and entertainment scene in the city while having supper at a neighborhood restaurant.

Day 7: Departure

- Visit one last site nearby or go for a morning stroll on Virginia Beach's beach.

- Take off towards the airport or keep traveling to other locations.

Note: This itinerary gives a broad overview of a few of Virginia's well-known tourist sites and locations. Your interests and the amount of time you have will determine how long you spend at each place. Additionally, take into account elements like weather patterns, seasonal events, and the accessibility of lodging and attractions during your vacation dates.

How to Customize your Itinerary following your interests

- Determine Your Interests: List the particular pursuits, points of interest, or topics that you find appealing. Are you drawn to Virginia's past, its natural wonders, its arts and culture, its cuisine and wine, or a variety of other facets?

- Prioritize Your Destinations: Look through the suggested route and choose the places that correspond to your interests. You could choose to extend your stay in certain places or make extra stops that suit your interests.

- A detailed study should be done on the attractions, activities, and events that are offered in each place. Find particular historical monuments, hiking trails, vineyards, art galleries, and other activities that fit your interests.

- Change Time Allocation: Change the number of days allotted to each place according to the pursuits you want to make. You may wish to spend more time at some sights or prolong your stay in a certain location.

- Include Specialized activities: Include activities that are tailored to your interests. If you enjoy outdoor pursuits, for instance, think about including a kayaking or hiking adventure in Shenandoah National Park. Include trips to famous restaurants or food festivals if you like eating.

- Examine Seasonal Events: See if there are any festivals or seasonal events taking place while you are there that would be relevant to your interests. This might give your route a distinctive and unforgettable touch.

- Choose accommodations that are close to the activities you have scheduled and that suit your preferences. For instance, if you like the outdoors, choose a cabin in the mountains, or if you like a luxury, pick a posh hotel in the middle of the city.

- Flexibility and free time: Leave some room in your schedule for impromptu exploration or leisure. To fully immerse yourself in the destinations and enjoy pleasant surprises, it's important to have some free time.

- Considerations for Transportation: Depending on your unique itinerary, make sure you have the right transportation plans in place, whether you plan to drive yourself, take the bus or train, or schedule private transfers.

- Please feel free to make changes and additions that reflect what you find most appealing about Virginia. Keep in mind that customization enables you to mold the itinerary to your unique interests and preferences.

XI. CONCLUSION

Embrace the Spirit of the Old Dominion: Final Reflections

As you set out on your journey through the Old Dominion, you'll learn more about Virginia's rich history, stunning scenery, and dynamic culture. Each region of the state has something special to offer, from the historic sites of Jamestown and Colonial Williamsburg to the breathtaking vistas of Shenandoah National Park.

Immerse yourself in Virginia Beach's charm, where the fun in the sun, sand, and ocean is waiting for you. Discover Chincoteague Island's wildlife and seaside charm, or visit Historic Jamestown to learn more about the country's early colonial history. Explore Norfolk's maritime heritage or Charlottesville's cultural fusion of history, art, and wine.

Explore the gateway city of Roanoke in the picturesque Blue Ridge Mountains. Enjoy the arts and culture on display in museums and art galleries across the state while admiring Natural Bridge's natural beauty.

No matter what kind of traveler you are—looking for outdoor adventures, historical exploration, culinary delights, or just a quiet nature retreat—Virginia has a variety of experiences to suit your needs. Keep in mind to embrace the Old Dominion spirit, immerse yourself in the community, and enjoy the distinctive tastes and traditions that make Virginia special.

May the beauty of the landscapes, the friendliness of the people, and the enriching experiences that have shaped your trip to Virginia remain in your memories as you complete your tour. Goodbye, and may your travels bring you many more amazing experiences.